14276
J
641.8
MOO

Moore, Eva
The Cookie Book

	DATE DUE		
DEC 18			
MAR 28			
SEP 22			
SEP 14			
FEB 11 '88			
MAR 7 '98			
FEB 5 '90			
FEB 21 '91			
MAR 08 '93			
MY 04 '95			

The Cookie Book

Also by Eva Moore and illustrated by Tālivaldis Stubis
THE SEABURY COOK BOOK FOR BOYS AND GIRLS

The Cookie Book

by Eva Moore

illustrated by

Tālivaldis Stubis

THE SEABURY PRESS · NEW YORK

To my own favorite cookie-maker, my mother

Contents

An important note to boys and girls who like to make cookies

There are twelve recipes in this book—one for every month of the year. Some of the recipes make crisp cookies and some make soft cookies. They are all different—but they are all delicious!

Here are some things to remember whenever you make cookies:

- Get a grownup's permission to use the kitchen.

- Read the recipe all the way through before you start. Then make sure you have everything you need.

- Wash your hands, and put on an apron.

- Ask a grownup to light the oven if you don't know how, or if you are not allowed to light it yourself.

- Always use pot holders to put the cookie sheet in the oven—and to take it out (of course)!

- Close the oven door after you take the cookie sheet out, and turn off the oven when you have finished.

Most cookies bake in a short time—10 or 12 minutes usually. They burn fast if they are left in the oven too long, so you must keep track of the time. Use an oven timer if you have one. Otherwise, check the time on the clock every time you put a batch of cookies into the oven.

After you finish baking, wash the dishes and clean up the kitchen. Then you may want to invite your friends for cookies and milk.

If there are any cookies left, store them in a cookie jar or some other container.

CRISP cookies should be stored in a container with a loose-fitting cover. (If they are shut up tight, they will get soft.)

SOFT cookies should be stored in a container with a tight-fitting cover. Put waxed paper between the layers of soft cookies to keep them from sticking together—and also between layers of crisp cookies if they are frosted.

When you read the recipes, you will see some words printed in italics, like this: *Grease the cookie sheets.* This direction and other directions printed in italics are explained in the back of the book, on pages 63 and 64. Look them up if you are not sure what they mean.

Cooking dictionary

SOME TOOLS YOU WILL NEED FOR MAKING COOKIES

mixing bowls

cooking spoon

measuring cups

Most sets of measuring cups include a 1 cup, a ½ cup, a ⅓ cup, and a ¼ cup.

measuring spoons

Most sets of measuring spoons include a tablespoon, a teaspoon, a ½ teaspoon, and a ¼ teaspoon.

sifter

There are different kinds of sifters in different sizes. A 3-cup sifter is a good size to have when making the cookies in this book.

cookie sheets

It's a good idea to have two cookie sheets. You can get the second batch of cookies ready while the first batch is in the oven.

pot holders

Thick ones! 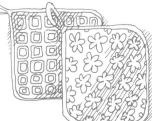 Or use two together.

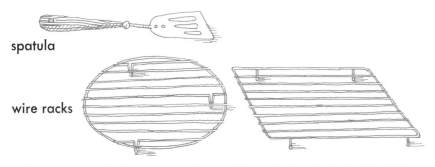

spatula

wire racks

EXTRA TOOLS YOU WILL NEED FOR SOME RECIPES IN THIS BOOK

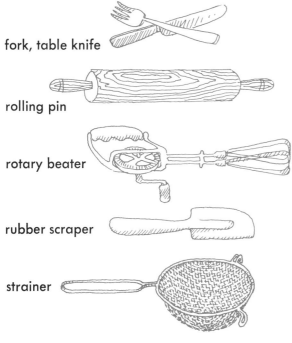

fork, table knife

rolling pin

rotary beater

rubber scraper

strainer

MIXING WORDS TO KNOW

stir

Move the spoon slowly inside the bowl to blend ingredients.

beat or whip

Move the spoon fast to blend ingredients quickly.

For other mixing and measuring tips, see pages 63 and 64.

January
Sugar and spice cookies

A special day for cookies: January 1, New Year's Day

Sugar and spice cookies

This recipe makes about 18 crisp cookies.

½ cup butter or other soft shortening
½ cup granulated sugar
1 egg
2 tablespoons molasses (light or dark)

1 cup flour
1 teaspoon baking soda
a pinch of salt
½ teaspoon cinnamon
½ teaspoon ground cloves
½ teaspoon ginger

1 cup confectioners' sugar (powdered sugar)

GET READY

Set the oven temperature to 375 degrees.

Grease the cookie sheets.

MAKE THE COOKIE BATTER

1. Get a large mixing bowl. *Measure the shortening* and put it in the bowl. Measure the sugar and pour it over the shortening. *Cream them together.*

2. Get a cup, and *break the egg* into it. Add the egg to the creamed mixture. Beat it with a mixing spoon.

Beat fast!

Stir slowly.

3. Measure the molasses and pour it in. Stir everything together. Stir well. Set the mixing bowl aside.

4. *Measure the flour, the baking soda, the salt, and the three spices into a sifter.* Sift them into a bowl.

5. Pour the sifted ingredients onto the molasses mixture. Stir until all the flour is mixed in.

14

SHAPE AND BAKE THE COOKIES

Use an "eating" teaspoon. (Not a measuring spoon.) One full teaspoon of batter makes one cookie. Scoop out a spoonful of batter and then push the batter off onto the cookie sheet.

These cookies spread out as they bake, so leave plenty of room around each cookie.

How many cookies do you have? 10? 12? 14? Put them into the hot oven. (Remember to use pot holders!) Close the oven door, and don't open it for 10 minutes. (If you have another cookie sheet, you can get another batch of cookies ready while you wait.)

After 10 minutes, look at the cookies in the oven. Are they flat and crinkled? Do they look firm? If not, let them stay in the oven two minutes more.

Take the cookie sheet out of the oven. Lift the cookies off with a spatula and set them on a wire rack to cool.

FROST THE COOKIES

Get a cereal bowl and a serving platter. Pour the powdered sugar into the bowl.

Take a warm cookie and put it on the sugar. Flip it around until it is covered with fluffy sweet sugar. Set it on the serving platter.

Dust all the cookies this way and set them on the serv-

All directions in *italics* are explained on pages 63 and 64.

ing platter. Then pass them around.

"Did you make these cookies?" everyone will ask.

"Of course," you will say. "I like to make cookies."

If there are any cookies left, store them in a cookie jar. Put a piece of waxed paper between the layers of cookies.

February
Coconut drops

A special day for cookies: February 14, Valentine's Day

Coconut drops

This recipe makes about 24 soft cookies.

¼ cup butter or other soft shortening	1½ cups flour
½ cup granulated sugar	1 teaspoon double-acting baking powder
1 egg	¼ teaspoon salt
½ cup milk	½ cup flaked coconut
½ teaspoon vanilla	
½ teaspoon lemon extract	

Maraschino cherries and extra coconut for decoration

GET READY

Set the oven temperature to 375 degrees.

Grease the cookie sheets.

MAKE THE COOKIE BATTER

1. Get a large mixing bowl. *Measure the shortening* and put it in the bowl. Measure the sugar and pour it over the shortening. *Cream them together.*

2. Get a cup and *break the egg* into it. Pour the egg into the mixing bowl with the creamed mixture. Beat it well. Keep beating until you have a smooth yellow batter.

3. Measure ½ cup milk and pour it on the yellow batter.

4. Add the vanilla and the lemon extract. Stir slowly around and around. Stir until there are no lumps in the batter. Set the mixing bowl aside.

5. *Measure the flour, the baking powder, and the salt into a sifter.* Sift them together into a bowl.

6. Dump the sifted ingredients on top of the milk mixture. Mix everything together. (Stir slowly at first.) Do you have a smooth thick batter with no lumps?

7. Add the coconut to the smooth batter and stir a little more. Now you are ready to shape the cookies.

SHAPE AND BAKE THE COOKIES

Use an "eating" teaspoon. Dip the spoon into the batter and push the batter off onto the greased cookie sheet.

These cookies will spread out just a little as they bake, so leave just a little room around each cookie.

Now decorate the cookies: Sprinkle some coconut on each one. Put a cherry in the middle.

Into the oven goes this batch of cookies! (If you have another cookie sheet, get another batch of cookies ready.)

Let the cookies bake for 10 minutes. The coconut on top will get brown. The bottom edges of the cookies will get brown. Time to take them out!

Lift the cookies off the cookie sheet with a spatula and set them on a wire rack to cool.

Put the second batch in now. Ten minutes later, take them out and set them to cool.

How pretty your cookies look! If you are having a Val-

All directions in *italics* are explained on pages 63 and 64.

19

entine party the same day, put the cool cookies on a serving plate. Cover the plate with plastic wrap or aluminum foil and put the cookies away until the party begins.

If you want to save the cookies for another day, store them in a container with a tight-fitting cover. Put a piece of waxed paper in between the layers.

Animal-shaped butter cookies

A special day for cookies: March 17, St. Patrick's Day

Animal-shaped butter cookies

This recipe makes at least 12 crisp cookies. The dough must be chilled one hour before the cookies are shaped.

½ cup butter or margarine
½ cup confectioners'
    (powdered) sugar
½ teaspoon vanilla

1¼ cups flour
¼ teaspoon salt

GET READY

Take the butter out of the refrigerator and let it get very soft.

MAKE THE COOKIE DOUGH

1. When the butter is soft, measure out ½ cup of it and dump it into a large mixing bowl.

2. Measure the vanilla and pour it onto the butter. Push it into the butter with the back of the mixing spoon.

3. Get a sifter. Measure the powdered sugar and pour it into the sifter. Sift the sugar onto the butter in the mixing bowl.

4. With a large mixing spoon, *cream the sugar and the butter together*. You will have a sugary yellow paste. Set the mixing bowl aside.

5. Now *measure the flour and the salt* into the sifter. Sift them into a bowl.

☞ All directions in *italics* are explained on pages 63 and 64.

6. Pour half the sifted ingredients into the mixing bowl with the sugar-butter paste. Mix them together with the mixing spoon as much as you can. It will be hard to do. Then pour in the rest of the sifted ingredients and mix some more. Use your hands to finish the mixing. (Did you wash your hands first?)

7. Put a plate over the bowl and set it in the refrigerator for one hour. While you wait, wash the dishes.

SHAPE AND BAKE THE COOKIES

First, get the oven hot. Set the temperature to 375 degrees. Then take the dough out of the refrigerator. Now you are ready to make some animals.

Get a cookie sheet. (You do not have to grease it.) Decide what animal you want to make first. How about an elephant?

To make an elephant, break off a handful of cold dough. Hold it in your fist for a second to get it warm and soft. Then plop it onto the cookie sheet. Press it flat with the palm of your hand.

Now use your fingers to shape an elephant. Push and pinch and poke the dough into an elephant shape.

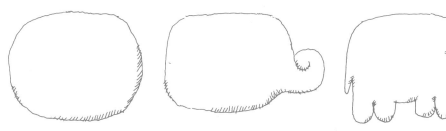

There is his body.   There is his trunk.   There is an elephant!

What kind of animal will you make next? A dog? a cat? a rabbit? a bear?

Maybe you would rather make flowers, or four-leaf clovers, or squares and triangles and circles.

It doesn't matter if some shapes are bigger than others, but try to make them all the same thickness. If some are thinner, they may start to burn before the thicker ones are baked. Leave plenty of room around each cookie. They get bigger as they bake.

When the cookie sheet is full, put it into the hot oven. (Remember to use pot holders.)

After 8 minutes, take the cookie sheet out. The animals should be brown around the edges but not in the middle. Carefully lift them off the cookie sheet with a spatula and set them on a wire rack to cool.

In a few minutes you can eat some animal cookies. Yum! They are crisp and buttery and good.

Be careful when you put these cookies in the cookie jar— they break easily.

Molasses cookies

A special day for cookies: April 1, April Fool's Day

Molasses cookies

This recipe makes about 24 soft cookies.

½ cup butter or other
    soft shortening
½ cup granulated sugar
½ cup molasses (light or dark)
1 egg
½ cup sour milk*
1 teaspoon baking soda

2½ cups flour
¼ teaspoon salt
¼ teaspoon ground cloves
1 teaspoon cinnamon
1 teaspoon ginger

½ cup raisins

*If you do not have sour milk, you can make some.
Put 1½ teaspoons of cider vinegar into glass measuring cup.
Pour in enough fresh milk to make ½ cup. Let it set for
10 minutes, and presto! You have sour milk.

GET READY

Set the oven temperature to 350 degrees.

Grease the cookie sheets.

MAKE THE COOKIE BATTER

1. Get a large mixing bowl. *Measure the shortening* and put it in the bowl. Measure the sugar and pour it over the shortening. *Cream them together.*

2. Measure the molasses and pour it in. Stir and stir.

3. Now get a cup and *break the egg* into it. Add the egg to the molasses mixture. Beat it up and stir it around.

4. Measure the sour milk into a glass measuring cup. Measure the baking soda and add it to the sour milk. Stir it around with a teaspoon and watch what happens—the mixture foams and bubbles up. Do you know why?

5. Pour the foamy sour milk into the mixing bowl. Stir some more—what a strange-looking mixture you have made! There will be a big change when you do the next step.

6. *Measure the flour, the salt, and the three spices into a sifter.* Sift them into a bowl.

7. Dump the sifted ingredients into the big mixing bowl with the molasses mixture. Stir it slowly. Stir only until the flour disappears. Do not stir too much! Now you have a smooth, brown cookie batter.

8. Measure the raisins and stir them into the batter quickly.

When you mix baking soda and sour milk, you get a gas called carbon dioxide. The gas bubbles up. Don't worry—it won't explode!

Carbon dioxide helps make the cookies high and light.

SHAPE AND BAKE THE COOKIES

Use a tablespoon or a soup spoon. One spoonful makes one big cookie. Dip the spoon into the batter and drop the batter onto the cookie sheet. These cookies stay in a mound as they bake, so you may put them close together.

Slide the cookie sheet into the oven and close the oven door. Wait 12 minutes. (If you have another cookie sheet, get another batch of cookies ready.)

After 12 minutes, look at your molasses cookies. Are

☞ All directions in *italics* are explained on pages 63 and 64.

they firm and dark brown at the edges? Then they are done! (If they're not done, let them bake two minutes more.)

Take them out of the oven and lift them off the cookie sheet with a spatula. Put the cookies on a wire rack to cool.

Taste one while they're still warm. M-M-MMMMMMM. Have another one!

May
Peanut butter cookies

A special day for cookies: the second Sunday in May, Mother's Day

29

Peanut butter cookies

This recipe makes about 20 crisp cookies.

½ cup butter or other
　　soft shortening
½ cup smooth peanut butter
½ cup granulated sugar
½ cup light brown sugar

1 egg
½ teaspoon vanilla
1 cup flour
½ teaspoon salt
½ teaspoon baking soda

GET READY

Set the oven temperature to 350 degrees.

Grease the cookie sheets.

MAKE THE COOKIE BATTER

1. Get a large mixing bowl. *Measure the shortening* and put it in the bowl. Then measure the peanut butter and put it in with the shortening. Whip them together with a mixing spoon. Whip them until they are blended together.

2. Measure the granulated sugar and pour it on the peanut butter mixture. *Pack the brown sugar* into a measuring cup and then dump it on the granulated sugar.

3. *Cream* the sugars and the peanut butter mixture together.

4. Now get a cup. *Break the egg* into the cup and then add it to your mixture.

5. Measure the vanilla and pour it in. Start to stir slowly. Then stir hard and fast until you have a smooth batter. Set the mixing bowl aside.

6. *Measure the flour, the salt, and the baking soda into a sifter.* Sift them into a bowl.

7. Add the sifted ingredients to the peanut butter batter. Stir slowly. Stir as hard as you can. You will have a stiff, light-brown cookie batter.

SHAPE AND BAKE THE COOKIES

Use an "eating" teaspoon. For each cookie, scoop out a spoonful of batter and push the batter off onto the cookie sheet. Leave a lot of room around each cookie.

Before you put the cookies into the oven, mark them with the back of a fork. Here's how you do it: Put some flour on a plate. Dip the fork into the flour. Then press down on a cookie with the back of the fork. Make criss-cross marks all over the cookie.

Dip the fork into the flour again and mark the next cookie. Mark all the cookies this way, and then put them into the hot oven.

Let the cookies bake for 10 minutes. (Get another batch ready if you have another cookie sheet.)

Ten minutes are up! Smell those peanut butter cookies! Look how much they have spread out! They are very flat and very soft. Use a spatula to lift them off the cookie sheet and put them on a wire rack.

Let the cookies cool for a couple of minutes. As they cool, they become crisp. Try one and see.

Everybody loves peanut butter cookies!

☞ All directions in *italics* are explained on pages 63 and 64.

Tiny timmies

A special day for cookies: the third Sunday in June, Father's Day

Tiny timmies

This recipe makes about 24 soft cookies.

1 small can (8¾ or 9 ounces)
    crushed pineapple
½ cup butter or margarine
1 cup light brown sugar
1 egg

2 cups flour
2 teaspoons double-acting
    baking powder
½ teaspoon salt

1 package (6 ounces) butterscotch bits
1 small package (about 3 ounces) chopped
    walnuts, or ½ cup whole shelled walnuts
Candied cherries for decoration

GET READY

Take the butter out of the refrigerator. Let it get soft.

Set the oven temperature to 375 degrees.

Grease the cookie sheets.

MAKE THE COOKIE BATTER

1. Get a small bowl and a strainer. Open the can of pineapple and dump the pineapple into the strainer. Let the syrup drip into the bowl. Set aside.

2. Get a large mixing bowl and measure the soft butter into it.

3. *Pack the brown sugar* into a measuring cup and pour it over the butter. *Cream* the butter and the sugar together.

4. Now get a cup. *Break the egg* into the cup and then pour it into the mixing bowl with the creamed mixture.

5. Measure out 3 tablespoons of the pineapple syrup and pour it over the egg. Beat everything together with a mixing spoon. Beat it well. Do not leave any lumps of sugar in the batter. Set the mixing bowl aside.

6. *Measure the flour, the baking powder, and the salt into a sifter.* Sift them into a bowl.

7. Add the sifted ingredients to the egg mixture. Stir slowly. Stir until the white flour is all mixed into the batter.

8. Dump in the crushed pineapple, the butterscotch bits, and the nuts. (If you have whole walnuts, break them into bits before you add them.) Stir it all into the batter.

SHAPE AND BAKE THE COOKIES

Use an "eating" teaspoon. One full teaspoon of batter makes one cookie. Dip the spoon into the batter and push the batter off onto the greased cookie sheet. These cookies spread out as they bake, so leave plenty of room around each cookie.

Put a cherry in the middle of each cookie.

Now they are ready for the oven. They will be done in 10 or 12 minutes. In the meantime, you can get another batch ready if you have another cookie sheet.

Time's up! Take the cookie sheet out of the oven. Carefully lift the cookies off with a spatula. (They will be *very* soft.) Put them on a wire rack to cool.

They look delicious! They smell delicious! They *are* delicious! Fit for a king.

☞ All directions in *italics* are explained on pages 63 and 64.

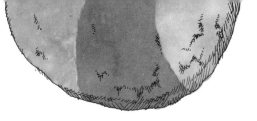

Three-color sugar cookies

A special day for cookies: July 4, Independence Day

Three-color sugar cookies

This recipe makes about 24 crisp cookies. The dough must be chilled overnight. Make the cookie dough the day before you want to serve the cookies.

½ cup butter or other
  soft shortening
1 cup granulated sugar
1 teaspoon vanilla
1 egg

1½ cups flour
1½ teaspoons double-acting
  baking powder
¼ teaspoon salt

Red and blue food coloring

MAKE THE COOKIE DOUGH

1. Get a large mixing bowl. *Measure the shortening* and put it in the bowl. Measure the sugar and pour it over the shortening. *Cream them together.*

2. Get a cup. *Break the egg* into the cup.

3. Add the egg and the vanilla to the creamed mixture. Beat well. You will have a smooth yellow batter. Set the mixing bowl aside.

4. *Measure the flour, the baking powder, and the salt into a sifter.* Sift them into a bowl.

5. Dump half the sifted ingredients into the mixing bowl. Stir and stir. It will be hard to do, but keep on stirring until all the flour is mixed into the yellow batter. Add the rest of the sifted ingredients and stir some more. You will have a big lump of sticky dough.

6. Now divide the lump of dough into three chunks. Make the chunks about the same size.

—Put one chunk on a plate or on a piece of waxed paper.

—Put another chunk in the bowl you used for the flour.

—Leave the third chunk in the mixing bowl.

7. Open the red food coloring and drip about 10 drops onto the dough in the mixing bowl. Mix the food coloring into the dough. Mix and push. Push and mix until the whole chunk of dough is red.

8. Use the blue food coloring to color the dough in the other bowl.

9. Now you have a chunk of red dough, a chunk of blue dough, and a chunk of white dough. Stick them all together and make one big ball. Then roll the ball of dough between your palms until it looks like a red, white, and blue sausage, about 7½ inches long and 2 inches around.

10. Wrap the roll of dough in waxed paper, or aluminum foil, or plastic wrap. Put it in the refrigerator overnight so that it will get good and hard.

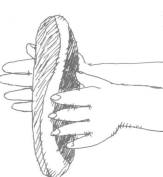

Time to do the dishes.

SHAPE AND BAKE THE COOKIES

You can make the cookies the next day, or you can keep the dough in the refrigerator longer if you want to.

☞ All directions in *italics* are explained on pages 63 and 64.

Just before you are ready to make the cookies, let the oven get hot. Set the temperature to 400 degrees. *Grease the cookie sheets.*

Now take the roll of dough out of the refrigerator. Unwrap it and put it on a cutting board or a plate. Slice the dough into cookies with a table knife. Make each one about ¼ inch thick.

Put the cookies on the greased cookie sheet. They will not spread out much, so you may put them close together — but not touching each other.

Let them bake for 8 minutes. (Get another batch ready if you have another cookie sheet.)

After 8 minutes, check the cookies in the oven. If they are starting to turn brown on the bottom edges, take them out. If not, let them bake a minute or two more.

When the cookies are done, take them out of the oven. Carefully lift them off the cookie sheet with a spatula and set them on a wire rack to cool.

These cookies look too pretty to eat — but they are too good *not* to eat. Crunch, crunch! Hooray for the red, white, and blue!

August
Oatmeal cookies

A special day for cookies: Picnic Day

Oatmeal cookies

This recipe makes about 21 chewy cookies.

1 cup flour	1 cup quick-cooking
1 teaspoon double-acting	rolled oats
baking powder	1 cup light brown sugar
½ teaspoon salt	¼ cup vegetable oil
½ teaspoon cinnamon	¼ cup milk
½ teaspoon ginger	1 egg

GET READY

Set the oven temperature to 375 degrees.

Grease the cookie sheets well.

MAKE THE COOKIE BATTER

1. Get a large mixing bowl and a sifter. *Measure the flour, the baking powder, the salt, and the two spices into the sifter.* Sift them into the bowl.

2. Measure the rolled oats. (Be sure you have quick-cooking oats, not instant oatmeal.) Pour the oats onto the flour. Stir with a mixing spoon.

3. *Pack the brown sugar* into a measuring cup and dump it into the mixing bowl. Stir the brown sugar into the dry mixture.

4. Now measure the vegetable oil and pour it in. Measure the milk and pour it in, too. Don't stir yet!

5. Get a cup. *Break the egg* into the cup, then pour it into the pool of oil and milk.

6. Now, mix! Stir around and around. The batter will be hard to stir. Stir with all your might. Stir until you have a gooey brown batter with no lumps of brown sugar.

SHAPE AND BAKE THE COOKIES

You will need an "eating" teaspoon to shape these cookies. For each cookie, scoop out a teaspoonful of batter and push it onto the greased cookie sheet. Leave plenty of room around each one. They will spread out as they bake.

Put the cookie sheet into the hot oven. (Remember the pot holders!) They will be done in 10 or 12 minutes. (If you have another cookie sheet, get another batch ready while you wait.)

After 10 minutes, look at the cookies in the oven. They should look like flat round cakes. If they look brown enough, take them out now. If they are not quite done, let them bake another two minutes.

Lift the cookies off the cookie sheet with a spatula and set them on a wire rack to cool. Be careful, they are very soft.

Into the oven goes the next batch! Into your mouth goes a warm, just-out-of-the-oven oatmeal cookie!

 All directions in *italics* are explained on pages 63 and 64.

September
Raisin-cinnamon cookies
or Chocolate chips

A special day for cookies: the first day of Fall

Raisin-cinnamon cookies or Chocolate chips

This recipe makes about 24 chewy cookies.

1 egg	1½ cups flour
½ cup butter or other soft shortening	½ teaspoon baking soda
	½ teaspoon salt
1 cup light brown sugar	
1 teaspoon vanilla	
2 tablespoons water	

1 teaspoon cinnamon and ½ cup raisins
or
1 package (6 ounces) semi-sweet chocolate bits

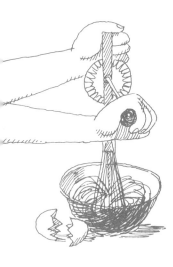

GET READY

Set the oven temperature to 375 degrees.

Grease the cookie sheets.

MAKE THE COOKIE BATTER

1. Get a small bowl and a rotary beater. *Break the egg* into the bowl. (No bits of shell, please!) Beat the egg with the beater. Beat it until it is light and foamy. Then set the bowl aside.

2. Now get a large mixing bowl. *Measure the shortening* and put it in the bowl.

3. *Pack the brown sugar* in a measuring cup and dump it on the shortening. *Cream* the shortening and the brown sugar together.

4. Pour the beaten egg onto the creamed mixture. Add the vanilla and the water.

5. Beat the mixture with a mixing spoon. Beat it until you have a smooth, creamy batter. Set the mixing bowl aside.

6. *Measure the flour, the baking soda, and the salt into a sifter.* Sift them into a bowl.

7. Pour about half the sifted ingredients onto the creamed mixture. Stir. Then pour the other half in. Stir until all the flour is blended into the batter. You have a batter that can be used to make two different kinds of cookies. Which kind will you make?

8. IF YOU ARE MAKING RAISIN-CINNAMON COOKIES, DO THIS NOW: Measure the cinnamon and sprinkle it over the batter. Stir it in. Then dump in the raisins, and stir them into the batter.

IF YOU ARE MAKING CHOCOLATE CHIPS, DO THIS NOW: Dump in the package of semi-sweet chocolate bits. (Do *not* put in any cinnamon.) Stir the chocolate bits into the batter.

SHAPE AND BAKE THE COOKIES

Use an "eating" teaspoon. One full teaspoon of batter makes one cookie. Dip the spoon into the batter and push the batter off onto the greased cookie sheet. These cookies will get bigger in the oven, so leave plenty of room around each cookie.

☞ All directions in *italics* are explained on pages 63 and 64.

Put the cookie sheet into the hot oven. The cookies should be ready in 12 minutes. (If you have another cookie sheet, get another batch ready for the oven now.)

Twelve minutes go by fast! The cookies come out of the oven! Lift them off the cookie sheet with a spatula and set them on a wire rack to cool.

The next time you try this recipe, you may want to divide the dough in half after step 7 and make half raisin-cinnamon cookies and half chocolate chips. Use half the amount of raisins, cinnamon, and chocolate bits.

October
Snicker doodles

A special day for cookies: October 31, Halloween

Snicker doodles

This recipe makes about 24 crisp cookies. The dough must be chilled for one hour before the cookies are shaped.

½ cup butter or other
    soft shortening
¾ cup granulated sugar
1 egg

1¼ cups flour
¼ teaspoon salt
½ teaspoon baking soda
1 teaspoon cream of tartar

1 tablespoon granulated sugar
1 tablespoon cinnamon

MAKE THE COOKIE DOUGH

1. Get a large mixing bowl. *Measure the shortening* and put it in the bowl. Measure the sugar and add it. *Cream* the shortening and the sugar together.

2. Get a cup, and *break the egg* into it. Pour the egg into the creamed mixture. Beat it all together. Beat it and beat it. Set the mixing bowl aside.

3. *Measure the flour, the salt, the baking soda, and the cream of tartar into a sifter.* Sift them into a bowl.

4. Dump half the sifted ingredients into the egg mixture. Stir with a mixing spoon. Stir slowly; stir hard. Then add the rest of the sifted ingredients and stir some more. You will have a sticky light-yellow batter.

5. Cover the mixing bowl with a plate and put it in the refrigerator. Leave it there for one hour. The dough will get cold and hard.

GET READY TO SHAPE THE COOKIES

Just before you are ready to take the dough out of the refrigerator, let the oven get hot. Set it at 400 degrees.

Mix the sugar and the cinnamon on a small plate.

When the hour is up, take the cookie dough out of the refrigerator. Get a cookie sheet or two. (You do not have to grease them.) You are ready to make the cookies.

SHAPE AND BAKE THE COOKIES

Be sure your hands are clean. Break off a bit of cold dough, about the size of a walnut, and roll it into a ball.

Then roll the ball around in the dish of cinnamon-sugar. Put it on the cookie sheet. Make more balls the same way. Leave a lot of room around each one on the cookie sheet.

When the cookie sheet is full, put it into the oven — slowly and carefully. Don't let the balls roll together. (If you have another cookie sheet, get another batch ready while the first batch is baking.)

Don't open the oven door for at least 10 minutes. Then look — magic! The cinnamon-sugar balls have become flat and crinkly snicker doodles! Are they brown at the bottom edges? Then they are done. If the edges are still not brown, let them bake for two minutes more.

These cookies are soft when you take them off the cookie sheet. Lift them up carefully with a spatula and set them on a wire rack to cool.

☞ All directions in *italics* are explained on pages 63 and 64.

November
Chocolate chip brownies

A special day for cookies: Thanksgiving Day

Chocolate chip brownies

This recipe makes about 16 little cakes.

¾ cup flour
½ teaspoon double-acting
    baking powder
½ teaspoon salt

1 cup granulated sugar
½ cup vegetable oil
2 eggs
1 teaspoon vanilla

2 envelopes unsweetened chocolate, pre-melted
(Nestle's *Choco-Bake* and Hershey's *Ready-mix* are two brands.)

1 package chopped walnuts (about 3 ounces), or
½ cup whole shelled walnuts

1 package (6 ounces) semi-sweet chocolate bits

GET READY

Set the oven temperature to 350 degrees.

Grease an 8-inch square baking pan the same way you *grease a cookie sheet.*

MAKE THE COOKIE BATTER

1. Get a large mixing bowl and a sifter. *Measure the flour, the baking powder, and the salt into the sifter.* Sift them into the bowl.

2. Measure the sugar. Mix it into the sifted ingredients.

3. Measure the ½ cup of vegetable oil and pour it into the center of the sifted ingredients. Do not stir yet.

4. Get a cup and *break two eggs* into it. Pour the eggs into the mixing bowl. Do not stir yet.

5. Add the vanilla. Add the pre-melted chocolate. Now, stir. Stir slowly at first; then beat well. Beat until you have a smooth dark-brown batter.

6. If you have a package of chopped nuts, empty the nuts into the mixing bowl. If you have whole nuts, break them into small bits with your fingers. Add them to the batter.

7. Pour in the semi-sweet chocolate bits and stir. Stir until the nuts and the chocolate bits are mixed into the batter.

8. Pour the batter into the greased baking pan. Use a rubber scraper to get it all out. Push the batter into the corners of the pan with the rubber scraper.

BAKE THE BROWNIE CAKE

Put the pan into the oven. The cake should be baked in 30 or 35 minutes. It will rise up. The top will be bumpy, and the edges will look crisp and will have moved slightly away from the sides of the pan.

When the cake is done, take the pan out of the oven and put it on a wire rack. Let it cool for 15 or 20 minutes. Then cut the cake into 16 little Brownies with a table knife. Cut one for your mother, one for your father, one for your sister, one for your brother, one for your best friend, one for you! (The rest for the cookie jar!)

 All directions in *italics* are explained on pages 63 and 64.

Christmas cookies

A special day for cookies: December 25, Christmas Day

Christmas cookies

This recipe makes at least 9 big cookies to hang on the Christmas tree as ornaments or to eat. The dough must be chilled for two hours before the cookies are made.

⅔ cup of butter or other soft shortening
1 cup granulated sugar
1 egg
¾ teaspoon vanilla

2¼ cups flour
¾ teaspoon double-acting baking powder
¼ teaspoon salt
½ teaspoon nutmeg

Here are the things you will need to decorate these cookies.
Frosting: You can buy ready-made frosting in a can, or you can make your own with 1 cup confectioners' sugar (powdered sugar), 2 tablespoons milk, and food coloring.
Cake and cookie decorations: Use colorful non-pareils, candy silver dots, red and green sugar-sparkles, and other decorations—it's up to you!
You will also need: plain paper, a pencil, scissors.

MAKE THE COOKIE DOUGH

1. Get a large mixing bowl. *Measure the shortening* and put it in the bowl. Measure the sugar and pour it over the shortening. *Cream* them together.

2. Get a cup. *Break the egg* into the cup and pour it into the mixing bowl with the creamed mixture.

3. Measure the vanilla and pour it on the egg. Beat the egg and the vanilla into the creamed mixture with a mixing spoon. Beat until you have a smooth yellow batter. Set the mixing bowl aside.

4. *Measure the flour, the baking powder, the salt, and the nutmeg* into a sifter. Sift them into a bowl.

5. Pour half the sifted ingredients onto the yellow batter. Stir with the mixing spoon until the flour is blended into the batter.

6. Now add the rest of the sifted ingredients. Stir with the spoon some more—then mix with your hands. Mix and mix. You will have a stiff, light-yellow dough.

7. Pat the dough down tightly into the bowl. Cover the bowl with a plate, and put it in the refrigerator for two hours.

☞ All directions in *italics* are explained on pages 63 and 64.

MAKE THE PATTERNS FOR THE COOKIE ORNAMENTS

While the dough is in the refrigerator, wash the dishes and clean up the kitchen. Then you have time to make the patterns for your cookie ornaments.

Get some plain paper. Draw a bell, a star, a Christmas tree, a stocking, and other Christmas shapes you like. (Nine or ten shapes are enough.) Make them 3 or 4 inches high. You can make circles too by tracing around the rim of a glass.

Cut out the drawings. These are the patterns you will use to make the cookie ornaments. Put them in a safe place until you are ready to use them.

BAKE THE COOKIE DOUGH

Just before you are ready to take the dough out of the refrigerator, get the oven hot. Set the temperature to 400 degrees.

Get a cookie sheet. (You do not have to grease it.) You will also need a rolling pin and a table knife.

Take the dough out of the refrigerator. It will be very hard. Use the table knife to poke the dough away from the sides of the bowl.

Turn the bowl upside down in the middle of the cookie sheet. Plop! The dough falls out.

Spread it around with your hands. Then pat it down. Push all the crumbs together. Push and pat the dough into a rectangle about 9 inches wide and 12 inches long and 1 inch thick. Pat it down well. Then—

Use the rolling pin to roll the dough flat. Roll up and down. Roll back and forth. Push firmly on the rolling pin, but do not push too hard or the dough will break apart.

If the dough starts to stick to the rolling pin, get some flour and sprinkle it all over the dough. Keep on rolling until the rectangle is smooth and flat with no bumps. It will be thick, and crumbly at the edges.

Now put the cookie sheet into the hot oven. When the dough gets brown around the edges (in about 8 minutes), it is done. Take the cookie sheet out of the oven and set it on a wire rack. Let it cool for 15 minutes.

MAKE THE COOKIE ORNAMENTS

After 15 minutes, take the cookie sheet off the wire rack and put it on a flat surface. (Use pot holders!) Arrange your ornament patterns on the rectangle. Put them as close together as you can.

Then cut around each pattern carefully with the table knife. If there is more room on the cookie rectangle, move the pattern pieces and cut out more ornaments. Make a hole in the top of each cookie ornament with a toothpick. Do not separate the cookies yet. Let them cool thoroughly first. While you wait, you can make frosting.

MAKE YOUR OWN FROSTING

1. Measure 1 cup powdered sugar and pour it in a mixing bowl.

2. Add 2 tablespoons milk. Stir. The frosting should be stiff. If it is thin and runny, stir in a little more powdered sugar.

3. Use food colors to color the frosting however you like. You may want to make half of it green and the other half red.

DECORATE THE COOKIES

When your cookies are cool, separate them. Work carefully.

Put the cookies on one platter and all the in-between pieces on another.

To hang the cookie ornaments, put a piece of thread through the hole and tie it into a loop.

Frost and decorate the cookies any way you like. After one side is dry, you can decorate the other side.

You may want to frost the in-between pieces too. These pieces are to eat; the decorated cookies go on the tree. Or maybe you would like to give the decorated cookies to someone as a Christmas gift. What a good way to say Merry Christmas!

Measuring tips...

measure and sift

First measure the flour. Spoon flour into the measuring cup and level it off with the spoon at the correct mark. Pour the flour into the sifter.

Next measure the baking soda (or the double-acting baking powder), and the spices: Dig the measuring spoon around inside the can or box until it is full. When you take the spoon out, pull it slowly against the opening so that you come out with a level spoonful. Empty it into the sifter on top of the flour.

Next measure the salt and pour it into the sifter too.

Sift everything together into a bowl.

measure the shortening

Dig out a chunk of soft shortening with a table knife, and put it in the measuring cup. Pack the shortening into the cup and level it off at the correct mark. Scrape the shortening into the mixing bowl.

pack the brown sugar

Brown sugar should always be packed tightly into the measuring cup. This is easiest to do if you use the cup that holds the exact amount called for in the recipe.

Spoon some brown sugar out of the box into the measuring cup until the cup is almost full. Then—with the back of the spoon—push the sugar down into the cup. Fill the cup again, and push the sugar down. Do this until you cannot fit any more sugar into the measuring cup.

...and other tips

break the egg

Tap the egg against the edge of a cup so that the shell cracks a little. Hold the egg in both hands and gently pull the shell apart with your thumbs.

Let the yolk and white slip out into the cup. You may have to push the white out with your finger. Make sure there are no bits of shell in the egg before you add it to your mixture.

cream together

This is how to mix butter or other soft shortening and sugar together into a creamy paste: Push the sugar into the shortening with the back of the mixing spoon. At first, the shortening will stick to the spoon—push it off and keep on mixing. Push and mix until the shortening and the sugar are blended together.

grease the cookie sheet

Greasing the cookie sheet helps to keep the bottom of the cookies from burning. It is easy to do: Dip a paper towel into some shortening or butter. Rub it lightly all over the cookie sheet. Do you have two cookie sheets? Grease both of them at the same time.